Charlie Custard

A Novel

With Added Custard

Greg Dobbins

Rhubarb Shuffle Publishing

CHAPTER 1

Warning!

This book contains lots of custard. LOTS of custard.

LOTS.

OF.

CUSTARD.

Look, picture the most custard you can possibly imagine. Now double it. Lots of custard, right?

WRONG!

That's still nowhere near how much custard there is in this book. This book has more custard than any other book ever written.

So, lots of custard then. But that's not enough on its own to write a book. Oh no. Unless it's a 'Cooking with Custard' book. Even then, you'd probably need a bit of fruit or something. So, what else has this book got in it, apart from custard?

Well, me. I'm Charlie. Charlie Custard, and I'm just an ordinary boy. Yeah, I've got a bit of an extraordinary name, but I didn't choose it did I? I come from a long line of

Custards. My dad, my granddad, my great granddad, my great great granddad... you know how it works. There was probably a Caveman Custard if you go back far enough. My name has just always been there, ever since I was born, so I don't know what it's like not to have it. It's just normal, to me.

You might think I get teased or bullied, having Custard as a surname. Well, you'd be right, a bit. The thing is though, my name is Charlie Custard, so what's the worst they can do? Call me Custard Boy? Yeah, that's my name; hardly going to bother me is it? I've been called that all my life, water off a duck's back. Not much rhymes with Custard either. There's mustard, but it isn't exactly any worse is it? 'Ooh look, it's Charlie Mustard!' Oh boo hoo, that hurts! So much worse than Charlie Custard.

So I get teased a bit, but not much. You see, the thing with bullies is they aren't very inventive. Unless it's an open goal, they haven't got the brain power to come up with anything decent. And with me the goal has already been scored, which confuses them even more.

So I'm just an ordinary boy, who fades into the background, and quietly gets on with the business of getting through the school day without doing anything to draw attention to myself, or stand out from the crowd. There's this girl in our class who dropped some of the banana she was eating one lunchtime, and somehow she sat on it without noticing, and it stuck to her bottom. She walked around the rest of lunchtime with it still stuck there. That was ages ago, like two months or something, and she's still called Banana Bum.

What else do you need to know? Actually, I'm very good at football, I should mention that. I'm small, but very nippy and skilful. I get kicked a bit, but not much because they can't catch me most of the time. I play out wide, taking on defenders down the wing, racing into space and crossing for my mate Big Mart to score. I don't score many myself, but I don't mind. We're a team, me and Big Mart. Big Mart lives just down the road, and we've known each other since pre-school. He's called Big Mart because he's very tall. Another inventive nickname, see. He is super tall though, almost taller than a grown-up. Actually, he is taller than some very small grown-ups. Not as tall as normal grown-ups though. He's like a big, goofy giraffe, always smiling. We're best mates; always look out for each other. He can do this weird thing with his eyes too, where he turns his eyelids inside out and it looks gross. It's cool!

I've also got a great imagination. My English teacher Mrs Griffiths says so. All of the other teachers just say I'm a daydreamer, but Mrs Griffiths calls me her 'little creative star'. Just goes to show, you can't please all of the people all of the time. I write loads of stories in English. Mainly about being a superhero, saving everyone from shark attacks, or killer zombie mutant teachers, or deadly poisonous wombats. I do write other stuff sometimes though, when Mrs Griffiths says could she have a rest from the superhero stuff. Then I just write about what it's like to be me. So the complete opposite of the superhero stuff. But she seems to like it. A real insight into my character she says.

I'd much rather be a superhero though. Like really, in real true real life. No-one would laugh at me then. Except when I told a joke after I'd saved someone. Like if I'd just saved Big Mart from a yeti chasing him down a mountain trying to steal his pants, I'd drop him off at home and say 'Ski you later, Big Mart!' Look, yetis just like pants OK, it's a fact. They get very cold, even with all the fur. You can't make these things up, it's in a book, so it must be true.

Anyway, I live in that house just over there. The middle one. With my dad, and my mum, and my annoying little sister, Emily. I'm standing here, on the corner of the street, with my ball under my arm, waiting for Big Mart to come and play footy in the park before tea. Sausage, chips and beans. Then apple pie and custard. Yeah, we do eat it, sometimes. It's not cannibalism, despite all the jokes at school lunchtimes.

I know superheroes usually live in cool ice palaces, or massive mansions, but I don't get enough money from my paper-round to buy a decent bike let alone a mansion, so there's not much I can do about it. Mum won't even let me change my wallpaper in my room. And she says you can't even get black wallpaper anyway. So I'm stuck with light blue, with pictures of footballers on it, which is good, but not really what you imagine a superhero having. Would pictures of myself looking cool in super-action be too much? Maybe. I'm not even a superhero though, so I don't know why I'm worrying about it.

Got to think about something while I wait for Big Mart though, haven't I? I could practise some football skills, but everybody parks their cars in the most stupid places, like right where the imaginary goal is on the other side of the road. Well of course their cars are going to get hit by my football if they park them there. Can't they see the big imaginary goalposts, right in front of them? Some people! I did come up with this other game to play, bouncing the ball and seeing how close I could get it to my face... that was OK for a bit, but I ended up with a nosebleed. It's just me and my thoughts then, until Big Mart turns up.

If I was a superhero, I could fly up into

the sky, and I'd be able to see how far away he was. How do you become a superhero though? Are there forms to fill out? Interviews? Do you get to choose what superpower you have? Maybe it's something I should look into, I'd make a cool superhero, I reckon. Don't you? Well, we'll just have to see about that then.

CHAPTER 2

And now here I am, hiding behind some bins. How did I get here, I hear you ask? Well, Big Mart turned up eventually. He's always late for everything. Always running up the school drive after the bell has gone, crashing into registration and getting sent to the office, again. Every single day. You'd think he'd just get up five minutes earlier, and get in on time, but he says it doesn't work like that. Everything he has to do just expands and still takes up too much time and he still leaves at the same time he usually does, and arrives late.

Anyway, he did turn up for footy, eventually. We ran round to the park, stopping at the swings on the way for a quick go, but the swings are all rusty and don't swing properly, so it was a bit rubbish. Big Mart was acting a bit weird too. He wasn't laughing at my jokes as much as he normally does, and believe me I was coming out with some whizz-janglers. And when we went over to the pond to skim stones he just wasn't trying. Three skims were all he managed, like something was bothering him.

'Something bothering you, Big Mart?' I asked. I'm good like that. 'Worried you'll never find a girl tall enough to kiss you?'

'No. Well, yes. But no. It's not that. There's something else I've got to tell you…'

'You haven't beaten my score on Alien Invasion 2 have you?'

'No! Look, I'm trying to tell you something important, Charlie,' he said, suddenly looking as sad as an elephant who's been told he's allergic to peanuts the day after he's moved next door to a peanut factory.

Well, my top score on Alien Invasion 2

was important. But I decided not to say anything. He clearly had something even more important he needed to tell me. Not that I could think of anything that could be more important than Alien Invasion 2. Until he said…

'We're moving house Charlie. A long way away. Dad's got a new job.'

Wow. Alien Invasion 2 really wasn't important, was it?

But… he couldn't move. We're… us. A team. The deadly duo. The terrific twosome. The phenomenal pair (note – that last one doesn't quite work, might have to think of something else). What could I say to show him all of this? What would Batman say if Robin told him he was moving away because his dad had got another job?

'When are you going then?'

'Couple of months.'

'Well… I'll… I mean, when you go… look, shall we go and play footy?'

'Yeah.'

Great work, Batman, you big loser.

We carried on over to the footy pitch, where a few of the others were waiting for us. We use my ball. I am the ball king. The king with the ball. If you have the ball, you have the power. Some of the others have got footballs too, but mine is the best, because my uncle works at the factory where they make them. So we always use my ball, and that means the game doesn't start until I get there. Unless I'm not playing, and then they do use someone else's. Although, this one time they forgot I was on holiday apparently, and stood around for about an hour waiting for me until they decided I wasn't coming.

Anyway, we split into teams, and the game started. We always pick good evenly matched teams, so it was a close game. It was 2-2, Big Mart had scored both for our team, and Lenny the Frog and Titch had got one each for them. It was nice to just be doing something, not thinking about Big Mart moving away. I still couldn't quite believe it. Football is good like that – all you can think about when you are playing football is football, there's no time for anything else.

Then the Thug Brothers turned up. I don't even know their real surname; they're older than us, and I've only ever heard anyone call them the Thug Brothers. Maybe that is their name. Not much stranger than Charlie Custard after all. Benny Thug and Bobby Thug. The Thug Brothers. If it is their real name, it's a good one, because they really are thugs. Big ugly bullying thugs. Bugly Bugs.

They wanted to play football. Not a problem really, except they always have to be on the same team. And that meant we had to switch people around to keep it fair. By the time we'd done that it was ten to five, which meant we only had ten minutes left before everyone had to go in for tea, so it looked like it was going to be next goal wins.

It was end to end stuff, with a bit of middle thrown in for good measure. And a bit of side, mainly me because I like to stay out wide. I got the ball near the halfway line, after Apple did a great slide tackle on one of the Thugs. I looked up and saw the other Thug charging at me. I pulled off a double drag-back nutmeg; now that is skill! I looked up and whipped in a pinpoint cross for Big Mart. He rose majestically to meet it and headed the ball powerfully into the goal. 3-2 to us, surely the winner.

I was just running over to celebrate when I heard this weird roaring sound behind me. I turned around and the Thug brother that I had just nutmegged was charging at me like an out of control wildebeest with his bum on fire.

'No-one shows off like that against me,' he shouted, spit flying from his mouth like a hungry T-Rex who's just had his dinner stolen.

Now, over the years I've experimented with various different strategies when confronted with an angry bully; standing up to them (not a good idea); joking with them (equally bad idea); threatening to set Big Mart on them (only works if they are smaller than Big Mart). The one strategy that I have found can always be relied upon, and that I chose to employ on this occasion, was to run. To run away. Fast.

So I ran away fast, only stopping to pick up my ball. Game over. Both Thug Brothers set off after me, probably feeling short changed as they'd only got to play for about two minutes. Now I'm quick, quicker than the Thuglies, but they've got stamina. Or stupidity. Or both, maybe. They just don't stop; when my lungs were burning and my legs felt like they were going to fall off, the Thugs were still there plodding away behind me. They probably just don't feel pain. I could taste blood in my mouth and it felt like my brain was going to come out of my nose, but there they were, still plodding away behind me.

Think Charlie, think!

I turned a corner and I was out of sight for a few precious seconds. Quickly, I darted down an alleyway between two rows of houses. I could hear them shouting, but I didn't look back. I dashed behind a couple of bins at the side of the alleyway, and ducked down behind them. I waited, listening carefully for any signs of approaching thugness.

And that's it, that's how I ended up hiding behind these bins. I think the Thug Brothers have gone, but I'm going to wait a few more minutes, just to make sure. They're not exactly quiet, the ground pretty much shakes when they walk past, so I reckon I'd know if they were anywhere near. I hate the Thug Brothers. If I was a superhero they'd be first on my list of things to sort out. So I'm more skilful than them at football, and quicker than them, it's not my problem is it? Why should they get to kick and push and fight everyone out of the way, but I can't use any little advantage I've got to try and beat them? Footy should be a game for everyone, not just the big fat cheating bullies. It's a bit like life, I reckon. Whoever shouts loudest or pushes everyone else out of the way always gets noticed. Bullies ruin everything. I'm fed up with it. I wish I could do something about it, but apart from occasionally showing them up at footy, what can I do?

If I was a superhero, I'd disintegrate them with my laser eyes, or drop a whole building on top of them, or dig a big hole in the ground super-fast when they were chasing after me so that they fell into it and got melted by the heat at the centre of the earth. Melting, meeeeeltiiiiiing... arghhhh. Simple.

I suppose they'll be after me at school

tomorrow now. I should be able to avoid them because they're not in my year, but lunchtime could be a bit tricky. I'll just have to hide in the library. Not much chance of them looking in there; I doubt they even know it exists. Plus Melanie Goodman is a library monitor, and she's lovely. My head goes all fuzzy and my eyes stop working whenever I see her. Yeah, I know I wouldn't be able to see her if my eyes stopped working, but you know what I mean; everything goes blurry and she's there in the middle totally in focus and beautiful and dark curly haired and smooth brown skinned, pretty and sparkly eyed. You know that feeling? Every single time. She smiled at me once too. I nearly barfed my lunch back up.

Right, I reckon the coast is clear now, so I'm going home for tea. I might have to wash my hands after hiding behind these bins though. Depends if I have time, I'm late already, Mum will probably be in a shouty mood now. All this and Big Mart leaving, it's not been a good day.

CHAPTER 3

I got home, and as expected Mum was in a shouty mood because I was late. I explained about the Thug Brothers but she wouldn't listen, she said I should have just left earlier. Oh yeah, annoy them five minutes earlier so they could chase me home on time, yeah Mum? That didn't go down well. She banged my plate down so hard the baked beans nearly hit the ceiling, honest.

So anyway, I started off with a bit of sausage, and then I had a couple of chips, the ones furthest away from the beans because they are still nice and crispy. Then I had a couple more bits of sausage, with beans too this time, because it makes them mush up better, and then I moved on to the chips that were covered in beans. They're almost like a different kind of chip, so really it was sausage and chips and beany chips and beans I was having for tea.

I wasn't in a good mood because of Big Mart leaving, Mum being shouty, and the Thug Brothers being thuggy, so I was thinking again how good it would be to be a superhero, so I could get rid of bullies like the Thugs, and never be late for tea, and make Mum really proud of me. Maybe I could work out a way to keep Big Mart around too. And you know, the thing with lots of superheroes is their name matches their superpower. Like Spiderman, he got bitten by a spider and got spidey superpowers. Ironman… um, is he really good at ironing? I've never seen that one actually. Batman, he has a bat cape, and a bat mobile, and well, loads of things with bat in front of them, a bat toilet probably, but I don't think he actually has any bat superpowers, so maybe he isn't the best example… Iceman then, he shoots ice out of his hands. Can't get more straightforward than that. Actually, does it come out of his hands, or wrists? I certainly can't think of anywhere else it could come out of. I guess it could come out of… ooooh.

Owchy wowchy.

No, no, no. Wherever it comes from, it must feel pretty weird, anyway.

So they get their superpower, and then they get their name. Or do they get their name, and then get the matching superpower? I was reading about something like this at school the other day. Nominative determinism. It means that a person's name can have an effect on what job they end up doing. So someone called Mr Baker is more likely to become a baker, someone called Mr Snow is more likely to end up as a weatherman, and so on. Makes me wonder why more teachers aren't called Mr Angry-Boringman. Anyway. The point is, if I wanted to become a superhero, then my superpower would have to be something to do with custard, wouldn't it?

At first, I thought that that would be rubbish. What good is custard in a superhero situation? But it can't be any worse than firing ice out of your hands, can it? And I wouldn't have to change my name, so Mum wouldn't have to sew new name labels into my pants or anything. Always thinking, I am. I'd just be 'Charlie Custard, SUPERHERO', instead of normal old Charlie Custard. I'd destroy the Thug Brothers, rescue kittens from trees, save a bus that was hanging over the edge of a cliff, and save Melanie Goodman from killer zombie mutant teachers, and she'd fall in love with me and we'd live happily ever after. Maybe we'd even smooch. Oh maaaaan!

The thing is, how would I get my superpowers? I've already got the name, and that hasn't made anything happen. I can't stare at people and blast them down with bolts of custard from my eyes. Believe me, I've tried. Something would have to happen to give me these superpowers. But you don't get custard spiders. And there isn't a custard planet in some far away galaxy that I could visit. Well, maybe there is, but even if I discovered it, it would be too far away to get to, unless I could bend space-time, and then I'd already have a superpower and I wouldn't even need the custard thing.

It was all a bit too complicated, and my head was starting to hurt. And then Mum brought pudding over, and suddenly it was obvious how I would get my superpower. Eating custard! I tucked into my apple pie and custard, feeling the custardy power flowing through my body. Yes, this was good. This was good. I decided to give my powers a little try. I pointed my finger at the floor, and concentrated hard. This was it, my destiny, my moment of glory.

Nothing.

Absolutely nothing.

I thought. No more custard left in my bowl, what could I do? I asked Mum if I could have seconds. There wasn't any apple pie left, but I could have some more custard if I wanted. Just custard – that was it! The apple pie must have cancelled out the effect of the custard. Yes please Mum, custard me up!

My second bowl of custard arrived. I ate a couple of spoonfuls. Finger point… nothing. Arghhh. Time to try a new tack. I checked that no-one was looking then dipped my finger into the custard, and left it there. I swirled it around a bit. The custard was quite hot, but I wasn't going to become a superhero if I couldn't stand dipping my finger in some hot custard for a few minutes. I stirred the gloopy, sloppy custard for a bit, feeling my finger getting hotter and hotter. I looked up and noticed Emily, my little sister, staring at me with a mixture of pity and contempt.

'Muuuum, Charlie's put his finger in his custard,' she said.

'Charlie, what are you doing? If you

don't want it, give it to your dad.'

I stuck my tongue out at Emily, and said that I did want it; I was just warming my finger up. Not my best lie ever, I admit. Mum said she was going to do the washing-up, and to take my bowl over when I'd finished. Dad went into the front room with Emily to listen to her reading. I tried my custard finger again. Point at the floor, concentrate, concentrate... nothing. Not a drop.

I glanced around at Mum. She was concentrating hard on washing-up the baked bean-y saucepan. I took a deep breath. Once I had my superpowers, this would all seem worth it. Quickly I lowered my face into the bowl of custard. Ikkk! One elephant, two elephants, three elephants, four elephants, five elephants. And out. Deep breaths. Clean the custard from my face with my finger. Mmmm, still tastes nice. That's a good sign. Another deep breath. Point finger at wall. Feel the power. Ready... wait for it... wait for it... NOTHING!

ARRGGHHHHH!

Why wasn't anything working? I took my empty bowl over to Mum. She looked at me oddly and asked what on earth I thought I was doing with custard all over my face. I was sure I'd wiped it all off. I told her my spoon must be getting a bit wobbly, and maybe she should buy me a new one. She looked at me even more oddly, but before she could say anything else I said I had homework to do (she definitely knew I was lying then) and went up to my room. I needed to think.

I thought.

Didn't help.

Then Emily knocked on my door and barged in. I don't know why she even bothers knocking. Little sisters are the most annoying creatures on the planet, even more annoying than panda bears. And boy, are they annoying. Not even real bears, are they. The grizzly bear… grarrrrr, raoarrr. The polar bear… roarrrrrr, growlllll. The panda bear… muh muh wah, bamboo num num. They've got nothing on Emily though, she actually enjoys being annoying. It's like her favourite sport.

'What are you up to Charles, you weirdo?'

'None of your business, Emiloo.' (I made that one up on the spot. Pretty good, huh?)

'So you are up to something, then?'

'No. Just go away.'

'Going then.'

'Go then.'

'Gone.'

'Good.'

'Great.'

'Grrrrr.'

I've got enough problems as it is, without Emily sticking her nose in. She's like Mum and Dad's little spy, always telling them what I'm doing… 'Dad, Charlie's feeding chocolate to the fish'… 'Mum, Charlie's running around the garden in just his pants again,' (it was hot, OK!)… 'Dad, Charlie hit me because I hit him but I only hit him because he was going to hit me and then he did hit me so I was right when I hit him so it's all his fault!' I wish I just had a guinea pig, like Big Mart has got, instead of a little sister.

I bet Superman never has any trouble with his little sister. And he always has his pants showing. I needed to get this superpower working, soon. Maybe I could do some research in the library at school tomorrow lunchtime. I couldn't give up now. And now it's the next morning. Nearly time to leave for school. I tried my finger again this morning, just in case the superpowers took a bit of time to start working, but unsurprisingly there was still nothing. So I guess I'll head off to school and see what happens today. I'll tell you all about it later.

CHAPTER 4

Good grief. A lot has happened today. Gather round, gather round... sitting comfortably? That's because you've got a **BIG FAT BUM**. Hahahaaaa! Good one yeah? Right, you're not going to believe what happened today.

It all started off normally enough. I got to school, whizzed across the playground at top speed, and hid behind the big portakabin until the bell went, so no Thug Brother problems so far. Lessons; well I don't need to tell you about them, you know how it goes. Yawn, blah blah blah, do this, do that, don't do that, definitely don't do that, bell, repeat.

Big Mart still wasn't looking happy, and I wanted to say something to him, but really, what could I say? He knows I'll miss him, and telling him that is just going to make it even worse. He'd told everyone else now, and they were saying how cool it would be in his super new big house, but they were also looking at me and I could see them wondering how I'd cope without Big Mart around. I was wondering the same thing. No-one else liked all the same things as me. No-one else laughed at my jokes with their big, goofy giggle. No-one else stood up for me against big bullies like the Thug Brothers.

Ah yes, the Thug Brothers. I still needed to avoid them for the rest of the day. Lunchtime. We have our lunch before the bigger kids, so I could scoff away happily enough. I just needed to make sure I was done and clear before the second bell went and the big kids came storming in. I did it, easy. I'm a super-fast eater when I want to be. Three fish fingers, bam! Gone! Salad… well, I had a bit. Tomatoes, and a bit of cucumber. Got to stay in tip-top condition for this superheroing.

I scurried through the corridors and into the library. Safety. No sign of Melanie

Goodman, but at the moment she was only second on my list of priorities. She was hardly going to fall in love with me if I got my face pounded by the Thug Brothers and ended up looking like... well, like the Thug Brothers, actually. So number one on the to-do list was avoiding the Thuglies. I headed for the science section of the library. Double hidden. Even if they knew where the library was, they'd never look in the science section. That would be like a tiger wandering into a restaurant and heading for the salad bar. Not going to happen.

I started looking through the shelves of books, trying to find anything that might have some instructions on how to become a superhero. It wasn't going well. There was loads of stuff about nuclear reactions, and chemical formulas, but it all seemed to be really bad for you. Like, death bad for you. It's kind of strange that there is so much stuff out there that is incredibly bad for you. Like the world is a big massive sweetshop and every other jar is deadly poison. That's no way to run a business. There I was, searching for the answer, when I saw her, walking through Poetry, heading towards Travel. Who? Keep up! Melanie Goodman of course.

I spotted her in Poetry,

And went weak at the knee.

My throat filled with gravel,

As she moved towards Travel.

My heart beating like a piston,

As she moved through the Dewey Decimal
System.

My heart's desire, my one true love…

Hold on, isn't that an Ugly Thug?!!

Oh no, this was bad, this was really bad. And I'm not just talking about the poem. Thug in the Library!

DANGER, DANGER!

Like a zebra on a rollercoaster, he had a look of confusion on his face; not really understanding quite where he was, but with a definite feeling that he didn't belong there. I ducked out of sight. So I had eyeball (a cool spy word for when you can see someone) on one Thug, but I didn't know where the other one was. I needed to be on my guard. I crawled along the aisle, and across into Travel.

If I could get through Travel and down to the end of Fiction, I'd just have to turn left at Nature and I'd be at the exit, and freedom. I kept low and crawled fast, glancing through the shelves as I went, on the lookout for Thugs. Then… clonk. My head hit something. I slowly moved my head up. Shoes. Tights. Skirt. A girl then. Probably. Oh my! Melanie Goodman.

'What are you doing?' she said, half-smirking.

'Dropped my pen,' I lied, not very well, turning bright red.

Her smirk moved towards three-quarters. I stood up, and heard a shout.

'There he is!' The Thugs!

Melanie scowled at them. 'No shouting in the library.'

I took my chance and dashed for the door. Down the stairs and out into the playground, then behind the portakabin again. Only five minutes to hold out, I hoped I could make it. I was low on provisions, and there was no clean drinking water, but I was shaded from the heat of the midday sun and hopeful I could navigate my way back to civilization without further incident.

'Oh Custaaard!'

'Oh no!'

Both Thugs stood in front of me, pounding their fists into their hands like wrestlers do on TV. I dodged left, but my path was blocked. I dodged right, but they moved again. I tried to go straight through the middle, but they both stuck an arm out and grabbed me.

'You need to be taught a lesson, Custard Pants.'

Well, a bit of effort on the name I suppose. And the lesson thing was a nice touch, what with us being at school and everything. I decided to just think this, rather than say it. Refer back to my joking with bullies remarks earlier.

'Got your stupid girlfriend to tell us off for shouting in the library too, didn't you, Custard Pants?'

Girlfriend? Wait, they meant Melanie Goodman. Melanie Goodman, my girlfriend? Yeah, I'll take that. I could still do without the custard pants thing, and they called her stupid, but I let that go. She did look amazing, as usual. Even from down on the floor, even when she was clearly trying not to laugh at me. She had a little dimple in her cheek where her lips were curving slightly up in a smirk. Her lips... Oh maaaan!

I was so lost in my thoughts I didn't see the fist heading for my arm.

THUD!

'Hurr hurr, dead arm for you Custard.'

'Stop it, leave me alone!'

'Nope. It's fun, hurr hurr.'

THUD.

I was getting angry now. I might be small, but I've got a big temper sometimes.

THUD.

Angrier.

THUD.

Fuming.

THUD.

Brain is boiling. Had enough.

'**STOP IT!**' I shouted. '**STOP IT YOU BIG IDIOTS.**'

Uh oh.

THUD!!!!

'Leave me alone,' I shouted, pulling my arm out of their grasp. I'd had enough. I'd been bullied by the Thug Brothers for too long. It wasn't fair, and it was time I did something about it. And they'd called Melanie Goodman stupid.

'**YOU'RE JUST BIG BULLIES!**' I roared, thrusting my finger towards them in anger. Anger, boiling up from deep down inside me, the flames fanned by the pain in my arm. Anger, burning at Melanie Goodman being called stupid. Anger, flaring against the hot salty tears that were forming in my eyes. Anger, that was shooting down my arm and forming in my clenched fist. Anger, that was making my fist burn, and my arm vibrate. Anger that shot out of my fist in a great stream of custard, splattering all over the Thugs.

Pretty cool huh? We stood there in stunned silence for what seemed like five minutes.

.

.

.

.

.

.

.

.

.

Then my brain started working again, and it liked what it saw.

This is fun, Thug One.

POW!

Custard straight to the face.

Now you, Thug Two.

POW!

Right in the stomach.

Both hands at the same time now, does it work?

'Duck!'

'Where?'

POW!

         POW!

Two for the price of one.

The Thug Brothers stared at me, custard slipping and slopping from their ugly faces. What are you going to do now Bugly Bugs? Charlie Custard is in town.

THUD!

Right on my nose. I felt a searing pain, the world turned grey and blurry, and blood dripped out of my nose, mixing with the custard the punch had left behind on my top lip.

'Freak.'

It turns out that being covered in custard doesn't stop a bully being a bully. It just makes them a custard covered, even angrier bully. One more kick to my thigh, and they were gone. I lay on the floor, a dead leg and a dead arm, blood still dripping from my nose, surrounded in custard. This wasn't how it was meant to be. I was a superhero, with a superpower. Nothing was meant to get in my way. The Thug Brothers were meant to run away in fright at my awesome power. Instead, I just got a slightly more custardy punch than normal. I struggled to my feet, disconsolate, confused, and a bit custardy, wondering what I had become.

CHAPTER 5

The afternoon at school passed in a daze. (Not much different to usual there then.) I spent quite a bit of time staring at my hands. There wasn't any sign of custard on them at all, and I couldn't work out where the custard could have come from. It just sort of appeared from nowhere. Apart from a bit of a burning and tingling sensation when I clenched my fist, I didn't really feel it at all.

I trudged home at the end of the day, downhearted, a complete dejectosaurus. Big Mart asked what was wrong, but I didn't want to reveal my secret power. Not when it was so useless. I also still didn't know what to say to him about moving away. I just didn't want him to; it was as simple as that. Every time I even thought about it, I could feel my eyes welling up with tears. I couldn't cry. Definitely not in front of Big Mart. Neither of us had seen the other cry since I'd dropped my ice cream at playgroup, years ago. So I didn't say anything. I told him I'd eaten my lunch a bit too fast, and still felt a bit sick. When I got home, I gave him my ball and said I didn't feel like playing footy that night, so he could take it. I had some more thinking to do.

Who knew that being a superhero took so much thinking? You've got the superpower, you save people, that's what it should be like. You're not meant to get beaten up after you get the superpower. You're definitely not meant to get beaten up because of the superpower.

But there we are. I'd got this superpower now, so I had to work out how I could use it. Actually, I wasn't entirely sure that I did still have my superpower. I hadn't dared try to fire anymore custard since the Thug Brothers unpleasantness. I decided I'd better give it another go. I took a football out into the garden, telling Mum I was going for a kick about (we've got loads of balls at home; I'd just given Big Mart my best one). I went up to the far end of the garden, behind the garden shed, out of sight.

Right. Test Number Two.

I pointed a clenched fist at the shed, and concentrated, hard.

POW. SPLAT!

Splurge, slop, slap, slurrrrpppp.

It worked! It still worked! Alright, it was still pretty useless, but it did work. And useless as it was, it was still pretty cool to be able to fire custard out of my hand. I tried it again.

POW. SPLAT!

POW. SPLAT!

Take that, evil bullies.

Except. Except, it obviously didn't stop bullies at all. It just made them angrier. I needed something other than just firing custard out of my hand. But that was all I could do. And it wasn't even hot custard. Not even slightly warm custard. Cold custard. I fired one more desultory shot at the shed.

POW.

SPLAT.

As I turned to walk back inside, I heard a creaking sound. I turned back to look at the shed, just in time to see the guttering dislodge from one end of the roof, and swing downwards. It hit one of Dad's garden gnomes square in the face and knocked him straight into the fishpond with a splash.

Now this was interesting. Very interesting. The shots of custard must have shaken the shed and dislodged the guttering. A little light came back on in my superhero dream world. The custard itself may not be any good as a weapon, but if I used it cleverly I could do all sorts of things. I'd been too simplistic, custard in the face was never going to stop a bully, but custard onto plank, onto cannonball, onto head would knock any Ugly Thug over.

I was excited now, my enthusiasm renewed. I ran into the shed and burrowed around, looking for things I could use for target practice. An old bucket, perfect. If I was going to use the custard to knock other things into action, I needed to be sure I was a good enough shot. A punctured football. A garden gnome. A plank of wood. A cricket stump.

I took my targets out and positioned them around the garden behind the shed. I stood in the middle and rolled my shoulders. Let's get this show on the road.

SPLAT! CLANG!

Straight in the bucket. That was pretty easy.

SPLAT! THWUMP!

The punctured football took the full force of a custard bomb and rolled over a couple of times, dripping cold yellow custard onto the grey paving slab beneath.

SPLAT! CLUNK!

The gnome fell over, and his head fell off, rolling along the path. Targets getting smaller now. I was confident though, I felt like I couldn't miss. I ran towards the plank of wood, which was balanced on top of a fencepost. I jumped and spun in mid-air, firing exuberantly over my shoulder.

SPLAT! CLATTER!

The plank spun around and tumbled off the fencepost. Just the cricket stump to go now, the smallest target of all. I took a deep breath, and aimed my finger straight at it.

SPLAT! HOWZAT!

I danced around the garden. I'd done it… Then I stopped dancing. Emily was standing at the door of the house, looking at me. Smiling.

'Ooh, dancing now, Charles?'

'Go. Away.'

'No. What are you doing? At least

you've got all your clothes on this time. Charlie! You've broken Mum's garden gnome. You're going to be in sooo much trouble. I'm telling. Muuuummmm…'

Great. That was all I needed. Still, at least my superpower was sorted out now. I'd done it! I did another much smaller, private dance, and looked around. Done what exactly? My euphoria disappeared as quickly as it had arrived. I'd hit a few targets in my back garden with custard. It still didn't really solve the problem of how I could actually use my superpower. Unless there happened to be a garden gnome handily balanced just above the head of my tormentor. Which was fairly unlikely, unless we were in a garden centre, and even then the gnomes tend to be at ground level generally. Still, I tried to be positive. I was in a better position than I had been previously; I'd at least found a possible use for my custard superpower. Surely there were other ways I could use it too; I just needed to work out exactly what they were.

I went back into the house, avoiding Mum, and up to my room. I got some paper and a pen, and sat down to write a list of

ways that firing custard out of my hands
could be useful.

1.   Shooting at things and knocking them over.

2.   Creating slippy pools of custard to make people slip over, if they're chasing me. Or if I just don't like them.

3.   Confusing pigs.

4.   Freeing young children who have got their head stuck between railings.

5.   Creating a distraction when I need to make a quick getaway.

6.   Impressing Melanie Goodman. Not sure how yet.

7.   Feeding hungry people. As long as they like custard.

8.   I love Melanie Goodman.

9.   Would she go out with me if I asked her?

10.   Do hedgehogs like custard? Maybe figure out a way it could help them cross the road safely.

11.   Something to do with a swimming pool. If they needed lots of custard, maybe for a charity custard swim?

I still had some thinking to do then. I'd just have to see what happened over the next couple of days, and see if any situations arose where I could try to help, with custard.

CHAPTER 6

Yeah, bit of a problem with the hero thing actually, sorry to be the bearer of bad news. It's been another weird day, let me tell you…

I kept my head down at school today, and avoided the Thug Brothers again. To be honest, I don't think they were even looking for me; I spent most of my lunch break in the library again, and they didn't come in there. And no, Melanie Goodman wasn't there either, before you ask.

Something was bugging me though. The Thug Brothers had seen my amazing superpower, yet no-one else in the school seemed to know anything about it. Normally rumours spread around the school faster than a cheetah on a motorbike who's late for a party. So why wasn't I being bothered by people wanting to see me fire custard bombs everywhere? Where were the crowds of people eager to be impressed? Well, obviously the Thuglies hadn't told anyone. I suppose it would sound a bit mad wouldn't it, telling everyone I had fired custard at them with my bare hands… and it's hardly good for their image, even if they did still beat me up in the end. Or maybe they thought I'd been carrying around balloons filled with custard, or some sort of hidden custard water-pistol, and didn't think I had a superpower at all? Hmm.

So it was just a normal day at school. Well, Lenny the Frog somehow managed to get a trombone stuck on his head in Music, but that's both pretty normal, and not something that affected me, so really it was just a normal day.

I was alert though, on the lookout for people in danger or in need of assistance, but apart from Lenny with the trombone, nothing much happened. And Mr Hunter the

Music teacher had pulled the trombone off before I had a chance to let the custard do the talking. The librarian had a squeaky wheel on her book trolley, but I thought an explosion of custard might be a bit over the top just to fix that.

So I walked home at the end of the day feeling a bit disappointed. It was meant to be my first big day as a superhero, and nothing had happened. I grabbed a quick snack, picked up my ball, and then headed out to the park to play football. Hopefully that would take my mind off things for a while. Big Mart was meeting me there because he had ballet first. Yeah yeah, a boy doing ballet. He likes it, he's good at it, and would you tease Big Mart about it? Thought not, you big chicken.

The usual gang were there in the park, minus the Thuglies, thank goodness. We split into teams as usual, and started playing, but I was finding it hard to concentrate. My mind kept wandering, thinking about my superpower, and how I could use it to support freedom and justice for all. I was staring into the distance when I was snapped back to reality by a shout, and turned to see the ball bouncing towards me. I didn't have time to react properly, so I just swung a foot wildly at it. I connected well, but not in the direction I wanted to. The ball flew over Big Mart's head (told you I hit it well) straight into a tree. It bounced around a couple of branches before it became lodged between a big branch and the trunk, halfway up the tree. Stuck, out of reach.

'Flippin' 'eck Custard!'

'It's my ball isn't it, what are you bothered about?'

'Yeah, well you can climb up and get it down then.'

Bit of a problem there; I'm not a great climber. Well, I'm pretty good, but because I'm quite little I can't reach that high, so things like trees are always a problem. We stood at the bottom of the tree, looking up at the ball. Big Mart got a long stick and tried to knock it down, but even then he couldn't quite reach it. He even tried a few ballet leaps, but he still couldn't reach it. That's how high it was. What was I going to do?

Yes, yes, you guessed it, the time had

come! This was it; time to dust down the superpower and blast that ball down from the tree. I stood at the base of the tree, looking up at the ball.

'I'll get it, easy.'

'You'll never climb that high,' said Titch. Like he's an expert on climbing suddenly.

'Not going to climb, am I?'

Everyone stood around me, waiting expectantly to see what I was going to do. I was going to amaze and astound them, that's what. This was it. This was my big moment, my chance to be a hero, my destiny. I rolled my shoulders and stepped forwards, concentrating hard on the ball. I slowly raised my arms and pointed my clenched fists at the ball, and then… I waited. Build the tension, give them some drama…

Once everyone was focussed completely on me, and they were beginning to wonder if I was going to do anything at all…

POW!

POW!

POW!

POW!

POW!

POOOOOWWWW!

Shots of custard hit the ball, **thwump, thwump, thwump,** and it fell down out of the tree. I'd done it; I'd really done it!

Except.

The ball fell down out of the tree, yes. Followed by a deluge of custard.

SPLAT!

SPLAT!

SPLAT!

Right on top of the watching crowd; gloopy, cold custard slopping down on their heads, and all over me too.

'Urghhhh!'

'That's disgusting!'

'Ewww, it's all cold and sticky!'

'Tastes nice though.'

'Smithy!!!'

Everyone turned to look at me.

'What was that Charlie? What on earth was that?' asked Big Mart.

'My new superpower,' I said. 'Do you like it?'

'Well, it did get the ball down I suppose, but my mum isn't going to be happy when I get home all covered in custard.'

'Erm, you might want to look at the ball,' said Titch.

We looked over at the custard-covered football, at the base of the tree where it had fallen. A family of crows from a nearby tree had flown over to investigate, and they had discovered that they liked custard. Specifically, they liked the custard that was all over my best football. They were pecking away at it, six beaks hammering away at the ball trying to get all of the custard off it. Then it happened. A crow pecked a little bit too hard, and hit the seam of the ball, and

BANG!!!

The ball popped, and slowly deflated, blowing a long, sad raspberry through the custard as it did so.

'Game over then. Nice one Custard.'

'Yeah, you big loser.' Lenny the Frog,

calling me a loser.

'Come on, let's go.'

I was left standing under the tree, with just Big Mart remaining. The ball had finished its symphony now, and was fully deflated, still covered in custard, still providing a tasty snack for the crow family.

'What just happened, exactly?' asked Big Mart.

So I told him, told him pretty much everything I've just been telling you (except the bits about Melanie Goodman). Once I'd finished, he nodded slowly.

'Not much of a superpower really is it?'

'Argggh! I know! But I've got it now, it's my superpower, so I've got to try and use it somehow haven't I?'

'Well, Smithy liked the custard,' said Big Mart.

'Smithy would eat anything. He eats grass when he's in goal and he gets bored. And anyway, feeding people cold custard is hardly superhero stuff is it?'

'There must be something you can do,' said Big Mart. 'I mean, it was pretty cool. Well, until we all got covered in custard and the crows burst your best football, anyway.'

'I just need some more practice. Get used to it a bit, like a new pair of shoes or something.'

'OK. Let's go to the playground and think about it then.'

Good old Big Mart. I knew he'd understand. We're a team, like I said. I must admit, I thought everyone would be a bit more freaked out by my superpower, it's not every day someone fires custard out of their hands; but this is a bit of a weird town, strange things do seem to happen here more often than other places. I guess that's why the book's set here – it wouldn't be much of a book otherwise, if nothing ever happened. I've read a few books like that before though, to be fair.

CHAPTER 7

Yes, pretty soon I got the chance to try and make amends, and show the world that my superpower could be a force for good. Here's what happened when I got the chance to try hero attempt number two…

We were still at the park then, me and Big Mart, and we'd gone over to the playground and sat on a bench, to have a bit of a think. Two heads are better than one. A bit of advice monster designers would do well to remember. Why aren't there any two-headed animals in the real world anyway? Surely there would be a big advantage for some creature somewhere to have two heads? Like sharks? Imagine that! A shark with two heads, full of razor-sharp teeth, patrolling the oceans looking for prey.

'Gnash, gnash, grrrrrr, raaarrrrrr…'

'Erm, Charlie, what are you doing?'

'Sorry Big Mart, I was just thinking about two-headed sharks.'

'Oh, OK… so anyway, about this superpower then. There must be hundreds of things you can use it for; we just need to work them out.'

We sat and thought for a while, but the bench wasn't a very thinky place. We tried the swings instead, but they were still all rusty and didn't swing properly. They weren't really swings if they didn't swing, should probably just be called 'Sits'. I don't know when they're ever going to get fixed; they've been like that for ages.

We went over to the climbing frame instead. Hanging upside down sends all the blood rushing to your head, surely that must help you to think better? There we were, hanging upside down on the climbing frame, when some little kids came into the playground with their mums. Little kids love swings, and they ran straight over to them to have a go. Well of course, the swings were rubbish, hardly swung at all, and the kids were getting upset. One of the mums was looking up at the rusted chain, trying to loosen it up a bit, and that's when it hit me! Well, not it, Big Mart, Big Mart hit me. Thumped me on the arm!

'Oww, whatcha do that for?'

'Your big chance! This is it Charlie!'

'What big chance? To get hit by you?'

'The custard! The swings! It'll get them moving again, won't it? Hero stuff!'

I looked over at the swings. It made my head hurt looking at them upside down, actually. I turned the right way up, and dropped down off the climbing frame, then looked over at the swings again. Yeah, Big Mart was right. All I needed to do was fire some custard up at the top of the rusted chains, and it should be enough to get them moving properly again.

THIS was it. THIS was my big moment, my chance to be a hero, my destiny.

I walked over to the swings and took in the scene in front of me. Two little kids, sat on two swings. Two swings that weren't swinging, because they were all rusty. All I needed to do was fire a bit of custard onto the top of each of the four chains, and the swings would be greased and ready to swing again. This was it, nothing could go wrong this time!

I told everyone to stand back, and asked the little kids to get off the swings. No custard dripping on heads this time, I'd learned that lesson. I took a deep breath, and pointed my hand at the first chain.

POW!

Custard shot number one.

POW!

Number two.

POW!

Number three.

POW!

Number four.

Four rusty chains, all greased with cold custard. I motioned for the little kids to get back on the swings. Go on, it's safe, Charlie Custard has saved the day good citizens. Swing to your heart's content.

The little kids climbed back onto the swings, and asked their mums to push them again. And, do you know what, it worked! The custard was perfect grease for the rusty chains, the swings were swinging again, and everyone was happy. I'd done it, I'd really done it, and this time nothing could go wrong!

Except.

The swings were swinging, yes. The custard was greasing, yes. But the custard was also gradually oozing down the chains, slipping slowly down towards the kids on the swings. So, a bit of custard on their hands, nothing wrong with that, surely? A small price to pay for the swings working again.

But the custard carried on slipping down, and it reached the seats, and it started to spread out across them. Two little kids sat on wet, cold, slippy custard, shouting for their mums to push them higher, higher…

S

     L

          I

               P!

Kid number one slid off the swing, and landed with a bump on the ground.

'Waaaahhhhh!'

S

     L

          I

               P!

Kid number two slid off the swing, and landed with another bump on the ground.

Another 'Waaaahhhhh!'

'Mummy, that boy spoiled the swings and made me fall off!'

'Mummy, I've got custard on my pants!'

'Charlie Custard, your mother will be hearing about this. Come on children, let's go home!'

Uh-oh! So close, so so close! Just for a moment, just that one little moment, I'd been a hero, and it had felt good, and then it had all been snatched away from me. Why couldn't I get this to work? This never happened in my comic books. Those superheroes never made kids cry, or got their footballs burst by hungry crows. It all went perfectly, every single time. And they never had to rush home for their tea.

'See you tomorrow Charlie, I'll have another think tonight, I'm sure we can come up with something you can do.'

'Thanks Big Mart. See ya.'

I walked home, fed up again. I'd got closer though, I'd nearly done something good. And that brief moment, when everything had been going OK, when I was the hero, well, that had felt good. And I wanted to feel like that again.

CHAPTER 8

When I got home, I got some old comic books out to read, hoping they would give me some inspiration. Spiderman first, one where he saves everyone on an aeroplane by firing a massive web in front of it to stop it crashing. Then Superman, one where he is walking down the street as his alter-ego Clark Kent, and then a bus skids on some oil and is careering out of control down the street, but he changes into his Superman outfit and dashes to the rescue.

And there it was. The answer. Why hadn't I thought of it before? I needed a costume! Of course! All good superheroes had a costume; it protected their identity, made them look cool, and obviously helped them be all superheroey somehow.

I pulled my dressing-up box out from under the bed, and started looking through. Spiderman outfit? Well, no, obviously. Same goes for the Superman cape. I'm not pretending to be someone else, I'm me, an all-new superhero. A cape would be good though. Maybe a yellow one. Except I haven't got a yellow cape in my dressing up box, just the red Superman one. I've got a yellow pillowcase on my pillow though. It's meant to be white, but Mum had a bit of an accident with the washing machine. I took the pillowcase off my pillow. Right, I had a cape then. Now what else could I wear? I rooted through the box again.

Pirate eye-patch? No, I needed to be able to see clearly.

Bob the Builder hat? What's that doing in there? That's not mine! I'm too old for that… it must be… umm… Emily's. Or Dad's. Yes, Dad's, that's it. It's not mine, what are you thinking that for?

Ooh look, cowboy hat and eye mask… hmm, that's more like it. That might just work actually. I tried them on, together with the yellow cape. I liked it. I liked it a lot. Charlie Custard, the Custard Cowboy, superhero extraordinaire. Oh yeah, this was definitely going to work.

Maybe I needed my pants on the outside too, like Superman? Couldn't do any harm to try, could it. So I took off my trousers. To save time, I decided just to see what that looked like, just in my pants. Not bad actually, though maybe I needed to stop wearing the Captain Courageous underpants. I mean, I'm the superhero now, aren't I. I was just admiring my outfit in the mirror, when disaster struck. Emily walked in.

'Weirder and weirder, Charles! What are you doing?' she laughed.

'NOTH… ING!' I shouted, trying to pull the cape around me and hide my pants.

'Nice pants. Again. Aren't you too old for playing dressing up though?'

'It's not dressing up. It's… it's for a school project.'

'Oh yeah, what's it about? How to be a donut?'

'Just go away!'

'Going.'

'Go then.'

'Gone then.'

'Good.'

'Great.'

'Grrrrr.'

A guinea pig wouldn't laugh at my pants.

I couldn't let Emily distract me from my destiny though. One day, she'd be sorry she ever laughed at me stood in my Captain Courageous pants, wearing a cowboy hat and an eye mask, with my pillowcase as a cape. One day! I packed the outfit into my school bag ready for the next day, and fell asleep dreaming of finally being a superhero.

*

Big Mart was full of enthusiasm at school the next morning. When he eventually turned up, late as ever. At morning break, he caught up with me on the way out to the playground, and reeled off a list of superhero ideas he'd had. Exactly the same as my list. Exactly the same. Even the bit about impressing Melanie Goodman; I didn't think anyone had noticed the way I looked at her.

Another yawn your pants off morning, Geography first, and then double Maths after morning break. Not much call for superhero work in Geography or double Maths. I decided to forget about it for a bit, and just enjoy a game of football at lunchtime. I didn't get much chance though, because halfway through the Thuglies turned up.

'Hey, Custard, why don't you fire custard at the ball?'

'Yeah, Custard. Why don't you… um… fire custard at the goalpost?'

Yeah, Great one!

They walked towards me. The game stopped, as everyone watched to see what would happen. I clenched my fists, wondering. But what could I do? I'd already tried firing custard at them, and it just hadn't worked. Then I felt a hand on my shoulder. Big Mart. He smiled.

'We're a team, right?'

The Thuglies stopped, and looked at Big Mart and me. Cogs were turning. You could almost see the steam coming out of their ears. Big Mart was big. But so were they. And there were two of them, and only one Big Mart. Plus me. Two versus one and a half. This was maths even they could manage. They shrugged, and carried on towards us. Big Mart bravely stepped forwards in front of me, but the Thugs just pushed him out of the way.

They picked me up, actually picked me up, and carried me over to the bins. You can see where this is going, right? Dumped, right on top of yesterday's lunch leftovers. Chicken curry, banana peel, bits of flapjack. Was that monkey brain? Oh, a mushy strawberry. Not much better. I scrabbled to get out, but then Big Mart joined me, thrown in by the Thugs too. They'd picked up Big Mart and thrown him in the bin! We climbed out, to see them strutting back across the playground like they owned it. Which in a way, they did. No-one in the whole school dared to argue with them. Even most of the teachers. As they walked past Titch, they pushed him over and took the ball from him. Thug One threw it in the air and swung a big booted thug foot at it. He connected with a thump, and the ball flew over the fence and into the street outside. They walked off laughing, over to some Year Ones, no doubt to collect any left over lunch money from them.

I looked at Big Mart. He looked at me. Then we both looked at the ground.

'Sorry, Charlie.'

'It doesn't matter. Thanks for trying.'

I didn't want to think how much worse it would be once he wasn't around anymore. I tried to think of the words to tell him this. To tell him how much his friendship meant. To tell him how much I'd miss him. To tell him that he was the best friend I could possibly ever have. But I knew I'd cry if I even tried. And everyone would laugh at me. At us. Friendship isn't what boys do, apparently. I just couldn't tell him.

'Reckon you can get the ball back with a long stick?'

'Might as well try.'

So we got the ball back, Big Mart holding a long stick, and me looking through a hole in the fence and directing him, until he managed to drag it up the other side of the fence and grab it. Team work, see. It works sometimes, just not against big bullies, it appears. We kicked the ball back to the waiting players, and the game got back underway.

Right at the end of the game, it started raining. Just before we got called in Titch did a mega slide-tackle on me, and we both got soaked in a great big puddle. We headed into school, grabbed our bags ready for the next lesson, and then went off to the toilets to get dried up.

We stood in front of the hand driers and tried to get dry enough to get through the afternoon, using paper towels to dry our hair at the same time. The hand driers just made the water warmer rather than drying us out, but it was the best we could do. Titch went into one of the cubicles to do a wee before the next lesson. I carried on drying off, and then looked at my watch.

'Come on Titch, we've got to get going.'

'I'm stuck!'

'Stuck?'

'Yeah, the cubicle door is jammed shut!'

I looked around. Everyone else was on their way to lessons now. I was the only person who could help. It looked like this was a job for... Duh duh duuuuuhhhh... Charlie Custard, the Custard Cowboy!

I ran into another cubicle and put on my cape, eye mask, and cowboy hat. THIS was it. THIS was my big moment, my chance to be a hero, my destiny.

'Don't worry Titch, I'll get you out!'

'Charlie, what are you doing?'

'Just stand back, I'll have you out in no time!'

I stood in front of the door, and took

the obligatory deep breath. Then the roll of
the shoulders, and I was off…

POW!

POW!

POW!

POW!

POW!

POW!

Volley after volley of custard hit the
cubicle door, rattling it on its hinges. I
carried on firing away, my eyes closed in
deep concentration.

POW!

POW!

POW!

POW!

'Charlie!'

POW!

POW!

POW!

'Charlie! **Stop!**'

POW!

POW!

'**CHARLIEEEEEEEE!**'

POW!

I stopped, and opened my eyes. The door was open. Hurray! I was a hero!

Except.

The door must have been open for quite

a while. Because there, still stood in the cubicle, was Titch. Covered from head to toe in custard.

'Sorry Titch.'

'Not the custard thing again Charlie. Just give it up!'

I got some more paper towels, and helped Titch clean off as best he could. Once most of the custard had gone, Titch looked at me again.

'Ditch the costume too, yeah?'

And off he went, leaving me alone in the toilets. I took off my cowboy hat and eye mask. Fat lot of use they had been. I went to take off the cape too, and caught sight of myself in the mirror. I looked so good. Why hadn't it worked? I reluctantly took the cape off, folded it neatly, and put it back in my bag. With custard still dripping from the cubicle door, I left the toilets, and headed off to my next lesson.

It was Art, so I sat down next to Big Mart and picked up a pencil. We were meant to be drawing a vase of flowers. Art is another thing I'm not very good at. I get great pictures in my head, but then when I try to draw them, my hand doesn't go where my brain tells it to and the lines come out all wonky. And flowers aren't exactly interesting to draw anyway.

As we drew, I told Big Mart what had happened before, in the toilets. And he laughed! Can you believe that? My dream is falling apart, and he laughed! I didn't see him coming up with any good ideas either. The costume had been a complete failure, Titch was in a mood with me, and I'd failed for a third time. Plus the Thug brothers were bullying everyone more than ever. And Big Mart was moving away. It was just too much to handle. I wasn't sure if I wanted to try and be a hero anymore. Maybe it was time to admit defeat.

CHAPTER 9

I thought having a superpower would be easy, but it's not. Nothing happens like it's meant to, and I keep making things even worse. It's been a disaster. So when I got home after school today, I made a big decision – I was quitting the superhero business.

I put my pillowcase back on my pillow, put my cowboy hat and eye mask back in the dressing-up box, and vowed never to fire custard from my hands ever again. Ever. The real world isn't made for superheroes. It just doesn't follow the script. That's the thing with films and books. They never show what the real world is really like. If you made a film with my dad in it for instance, it would just have him sat at a desk for eight hours a day staring at a computer, interspersed with occasional trips to the toilet. Can't see that winning any Oscars.

In real life, there aren't any happy endings. There are just endings. And most of the time, even those aren't really endings, they're just middles. Like me giving up the superheroing. It's not the end is it? I've still got to go to school tomorrow. I've still got hands that can fire custard. I'm just not going to use them anymore. I can hardly walk into the sunset as the credits roll after that, can I?

It's the school summer fete on Saturday too. There's a 5-a-side football tournament that I'm meant to be playing in. Maybe we'll win that. If Titch is talking to me by then of course. At least I would win something then. And if Melanie Goodman was watching, and saw me score the winning goal, and came over, and…

Oh, who am I kidding? That's what I'm on about; it doesn't matter how much you want something to happen, how much you dream about it, how much you wish and hope, the world just doesn't work like that.

After I'd got home from school, and packed away my superhero costume, forever, Mum shouted up and asked me if I wanted to go to the supermarket with her. Now, ordinarily I'd say no, because I'd be off out to play football. But this evening, well… I just couldn't face the lads, I didn't want to get into an argument with Titch, and I just didn't have the energy. I thought going shopping with Mum might be comforting. Maybe I could persuade her to buy some nice chocolate biscuits for once.

We drove to the big supermarket in town, and I asked if I could drive the trolley. Mum said yes, so long as I watched where I was going and didn't knock over any old ladies this time. Look, last time was just an accident, she was really small and I couldn't see her over the top of the trolley. She fell into a pile of toilet rolls anyway, so it was a soft landing. A double soft extra quilted landing actually.

I drove sensibly and at an appropriate speed around the supermarket. I would probably have passed my trolley driving test if such a thing existed. We had just turned through cold meats and into the fruit aisle when suddenly Melanie Goodman was walking towards us, with her mum. Melanie Goodman, beautiful as ever, framed by a stack of pineapples and a row of grapefruits. Now, my mum knows Melanie's mum, so we stopped to talk to them. Well, they talked, I stared. Until Melanie noticed and gave me a funny look.

So I looked at their trolley instead. Oh my goodness. Soup. Tins and tins of soup. Just soup. Nothing else at all. Not even any bread to dip in it. Just soup. I felt Melanie looking at me again, and my mouth decided it had better speak, but forgot to check if it was OK with my brain first.

'You sure like soup,' I said. Good grief. You sure like soup. I think I even said it with a bit of an American accent. Where had that come from?

'Oh, it's not for us,' she said, in her perfect, soft, lovely voice. 'We help out at the local soup kitchen for homeless people, down Burns Street.'

Of course. A soup kitchen. Of course it wasn't for her. What made you think that? I knew it wasn't for her; someone as lovely as Melanie eating soup? Get out of here; you're crazy. It was for the soup kitchen of course.

'What's a soup kitchen?'

'Well, a couple of times a week we serve soup to any homeless people in the area, to make sure they at least get one decent meal a day.'

Of course. A soup kitchen. I knew that. They give homeless people soup.

'What about pudding?' What about pudding? Good grief, come on mouth, at least think about checking with my brain before you say these things.

'We can't really afford pudding as well,' she said. 'It's only a small charity.'

Light bulb!

Do you see where this is going? Of course you do, you're very clever, I've always thought that. Here was a chance to at least do something good with my superpower. It might not be heroic and brave and amazing, but it was something good. Something useful. Once we'd said goodbye to Melanie and her mum and finished the shopping, and my brain had started working properly again, I asked Mum if I could walk home. She said it was fine because she had to pick Emily up from karate on the way home anyway, so she'd see me when they got back.

I ran out of the supermarket and headed in the direction of the soup kitchen. As I ran, I considered the different ways I could approach helping out.

Burst in through the door and tell everyone to stand back, before I blasted their bowls full of custard? No, too showy.

Stroll in and offer to provide custard for everyone, then start filling bowls up with my magic hands? No. Better, but this wasn't about me. It wasn't about being a hero, or showing everyone that I was helping out, or even impressing Melanie Goodman. It was just doing something good for other people. No-one even needed to know it was me doing it.

I saw the soup kitchen set up further along the road. It was just a big tent, with a table at the front holding big saucepans full of soup on three gas stoves. Melanie and her mum were stood behind the table, dipping ladles into the big saucepans and dishing out bowls of soup to a queue of people. I walked past, unnoticed, and then doubled back, darting behind the tent. I peeped in through a flap in the tent, and saw Melanie and her mum still stood at the front. Along the back of the tent were tins of soup stacked up waiting to be opened, and three more big empty saucepans. I double checked that no-one was looking, and then sneaked over to the saucepans. I knelt down behind them, and aimed my fist at the first one. I concentrated, and then, splat, splat, splat, splurge, slowly and carefully I filled the saucepan up with custard. I moved on and did the same to the other two saucepans, and then, checking the coast was clear, crawled out of the tent and ran off down the road.

I stopped at the corner and looked back. Melanie's mum had just taken away an empty saucepan of soup, and was lifting a new saucepan up onto the stove on the table. I saw the look of confusion on her face, and the big double-take, as she noticed that the saucepan was already full. And not with soup, but custard! I saw her speak to

Melanie, and saw Melanie looking into the saucepan too. Then they both shrugged, and started dishing out custard to anyone who wanted it. And quite a few people wanted it, let me tell you. I saw smiles. It felt good. Maybe superpowers don't just have to be about rescuing people and fighting monsters. Maybe it can be more subtle than that?

I walked home, happy. Maybe I'd been a little bit hasty putting away that costume after all.

CHAPTER 10

The day of the Summer Fete. Maybe
this would be my big chance to do some
proper heroing? I had my outfit with me in a
bag, just in case. The fete was raising funds
for some new library books this year, so the
Library Club had a cake stall set up in the
playground, along with loads more stalls and
rides, and the football competition was
taking place on the field.

And guess what? We got to the final of
the football, and won! I checked a couple of
times to see if Melanie Goodman was
watching, but she wasn't anywhere to be
seen. Probably helping with the cake sale. I

bet she makes great cakes too. *Sigh.*

After the football was over and we had collected our medals, we were free to look around the rest of the stalls. But to be honest, it wasn't that great. The cakes were wonderful, of course. How dare you think that I would even consider suggesting otherwise? I bought a triple chocolate brownie with double chocolate icing and chocolate sprinkles, from Melanie Goodman. And I'm sure she smiled at me, just a little bit. Problem was, that made my stomach start doing some serious somersaults, and I didn't really feel like eating my brownie after that, so Big Mart scoffed most of it, as well as his own.

The cakes were fantastic then. It was just the rest of the fete that was a bit of a let-down. Mr Miller was in charge of the Merry-go-Round, but the rickety thing was even older than him. And he's ancient, like forty or something! It was creaking and squeaking round at a snail's pace. And this snail had a bad back and a bag full of heavy books. It was so slooooooowwww. Honestly, kids were falling asleep on it, it was going round so gently.

The Coconut Shy was perhaps even more disappointing. The basic problem here was they didn't have any coconuts, which is quite a problem for a COCONUT Shy. So it was just a Shy really. Very shy. Kids were lining up for the thrilling chance to throw a wooden ball at a stick. I mean, come on! Throwing a wooden ball at a stick. For the chance to win… a balloon. Not even a blown up balloon either. The air-pump wasn't working. And that leads us to the biggest problem of all.

No air-pump meant… NO BOUNCY CASTLE! This was a disaster, with a capital **D**. A **D**isaster! Big Mart was trying to be brave, but his voice was a bit wobbly, and I swear there were tears in his eyes. Big Mart *loves* a bouncy castle. This was without a doubt the lamest, most sleeporific summer fete ever. Like really ever. Even cavemen must have had a better summer fete than this, throwing rocks at bigger rocks, for the chance to win an even bigger rock. The library would only be able to get about one new book at this rate, and Melanie Goodman would be really upset. Something had to be done. Something had to be done, by someone.

Me.

Something had to be done by me. This was it. My big chance, my moment to shine. I wouldn't be rescuing anyone, or fighting super-villains, but I'd be making everyone happy. I'd be the Saviour of the Summer Fete. I'd be… Charlie Custard, the CUSTARD COWBOY.

Back in town, and this time it's personal. Well, not really, but I've always wanted to say that.

I dashed inside, and into the school toilets. I needed to get changed into my outfit, but also I was so excited I really needed a wee. Once I'd done a wee, and I had my cape, eye mask and cowboy hat on, I stood in front of the mirror and pondered the pants question. Oh why not? It was part of the outfit, and today it wasn't Captain Courageous, it was dinosaurs in spaceships. Everyone loves dinosaurs in spaceships, right? Right? This was going to be amazing. I had it all planned out in my head, what I needed to do to make this fete a success, to be the hero, to impress Melanie Goodman.

I strode out into the playground. There

were gasps, presumably of admiration. People pointed. People laughed. Oh yes, they were that happy! They knew the fete was just about to get a whole lot better, now the Custard Cowboy was in town.

I started off at the Merry-go-Round. Or the Gloomy-go-Slow, as it was at the moment. Stand back kids, the Custard Cowboy is here to save the day. I'd learned a lesson at the swings, not to use too much custard. And here, the central pole just needed a bit of greasing at the bottom, so there was no chance of any custard dripping on anyone. I couldn't fail.

I rolled up my sleeves, and tipped my hat at the watching crowd. Hero business. Then…

POW!

POW!

POW!

SPLAT!

Enjoy the ride good citizens, £1 a go, keep your hands and feet inside the ride at all times. Oh yeah! I say Charlie, you say Custard. Charlie…

…

…

…

Um.

OK, maybe they weren't quite ready for that yet. But they were happy, they really were. The Merry-go-Round was spinning properly, kids were laughing, parents were smiling. I was a superhero!

Next up on my big list of hero assignments was the Coconut Shy. I'd had a humdoozler of an idea here. Roll up my sleeves again, tip my hat at the watching crowd. Hero business. Then…

SPLURGE!

SPLURGE!

SPLUUUUUUURGE!

balloon after balloon filled with custard. This was no longer a Coconut Shy, oh no, that's so last week. Here we have a Custard Shy! Throw the ball, make the balloon filled with custard explode. The prize? Mrs Marks, the stall-holder and terror of Year One kids for centuries, covered in custard. Truly a prize money can't buy. Roll up, roll up, £1 for three balls, keep your hands and feet inside the ride at all times.

This was going great. Like really great! More people were happy. Custard balloons were popping, everyone was laughing, even Mrs Marks was smiling away beneath the custard. Isn't it weird, seeing teachers out of school? They're like different people, happy, smiling, not even telling you off for running across the playground. What does the Headteacher do to them when they enter that building, is it remote control or something?

One person was still sad though. Big

Mart

. Sure, you can go on the Merry-go-Round, you can throw wooden balls at balloons full of custard, you can eat cakes and candy floss until you feel slightly sick and your eyes go a bit fuzzy, but it's not a fete without a bouncy castle. Not for Big Mart. Like I said, Big Mart *loves* a bouncy castle. So this was the big one. A going away present for my best mate.

Roll up sleeves, tip hat, hero business. You know how it goes by now. I needed to concentrate though, the bouncy castle was big. It was going to take a lot of custard to fill it up. I closed my eyes, preparing for my moment in the sun. Well, light cloud. This is a summer fete we're talking about, after all. Then…

SQUELCH!

SQUELCH!

SQUELCH!

SQUELCH!

SQUELCH!

SQUELCH!

SQUELCH!

(imagine about fifty more squelches here)…

and… TA DAAAAA! A Custard Castle! Not quite as bouncy, a bit more wobbly, but still lots of fun. £1 a go, take off your shoes, keep your hands and feet inside the ride at all times.

Big Mart stepped up. He grinned at me. 'Thanks Charlie.' And on he jumped, happy again, a big goofy giraffe bouncing up and down with arms and legs flying all over the place. I joined him, and we had a fine time. People were queuing up for a go on the Custard Castle. People were queuing up for a chance to thank Charlie Custard. I climbed off the Custard Castle with Big Mart, and shook hands with the watching crowd, all thanking me, all patting me on the back. The Custard Cowboy. The superhero.

Then, disaster. This time with all capital letters. **DISASTER**. The Thuglies, barging their way to the front of the queue for the Custard Castle, demanding a go, now! They charged onto the castle, and soon little kids were flying everywhere. Eventually it was just the two of them left on there, bouncing up and down and bashing into each other. Big ugly thugs. Should I give them a volley of custard? Knock them over and teach them a lesson? Was I brave enough, now I was a proper hero?

I didn't have chance to find out. They were bouncing higher and higher, harder and harder. And then there was a noise, a really loud noise, like a hippo sitting on a giant whoopee cushion.

FLLLUUUUURRRPPPPP!

The centre seam of the bouncy castle ripped open, and a huge fountain of custard sprayed upwards, lifting the Thuglies up, up, up on top of it. They cried out in shock, and then shouted even louder as the fountain stopped and they were dropped down into the huge lake of custard that was now spread out beneath them.

SPLAT!

Two Thugs, covered from head to toe in custard, scrabbling around on the floor. They kept slipping over, floundering around in the custard, legs flailing as they tried to stand up, pulling each other back over as they grabbed on to try and heave themselves up. I added some more custard into the mix, just for fun. That raised a big cheer from the watching crowd. Eventually the Thugs were up on their feet, custard dripping off them, looking furious. And everyone laughed. Pointed at them, and laughed, roared, clutching their sides at the sight of the two big bullies covered in custard.

I laughed too, but caught Big Mart's eye and signalled that maybe it was time to make a quick getaway. There's being a hero, and then there's just being stupid. My job was done here, time to run away, safe to custard   another   day.

CHAPTER 11

We scurried across the playground, well out of sight of the Thuglies, laughing as we ran. It's pretty difficult to run and laugh at the same time, actually. We stopped to catch our breath, and then I spotted her. Who? Really? Do we have to go through all of this again? Melanie Goodman of course! She was smiling, and walking towards us. Oh boy!

'That was great,' she sparkled. Oh yeah, she doesn't just say, she sparkles. 'Thanks, Charlie. You've really saved the day. And it was great to see those bullies getting their just desserts too.'

Big Mart chuckled a big goofy chuckle. 'Just desserts! Nice one!'

'Thanks Big Mart,' sparkled Melanie. 'I'm glad you're not moving house anymore, too. We'd miss your laugh too much.'

Wait, what? Big Mart wasn't moving? Why hadn't he told me? How did Melanie know? Did Melanie really just say I'd saved the day? Might she smooch me in a minute? Could I start breathing again soon?

'Bye,' she sparkled, snapping me out of it. 'See you at school on Monday. Oh, hi Emily. I was just telling your big brother what a hero he's been today.'

Emily strolled up to us, smiling. 'Was that your big secret then, Charlie? It was pretty cool, I guess. We could have done without the dinosaur pants though... But my brother, the superhero! Yeah, it's pretty cool. See you later. Bye, Big Mart.'

Always with the pants! Oh yeah, Big Mart. I still needed to have a word with him actually.

'So you're not moving away after all?' I asked.

'No. They said Dad could work from here. Do it all on his computer, or something, and set up a new office for them. We are getting a bigger house though, over on that new estate.'

'Why didn't you tell me you were staying?'

'I dunno. I wasn't sure you were even bothered. You hadn't said anything. I wasn't sure you even wanted to be my friend anymore.'

'Of course I did. Of course I do. I just… I didn't know what to say. You're my best friend. I just couldn't work out what to say, that's all, or how to say it. Not without crying, anyway.'

'I thought you were glad I was going.'

'And I thought you were glad to be getting away from me.'

'You're a numpty, aren't you, Charlie?'

'You're a numpty too, Big Mart.'

'Best friends?'

'The best. We're the deadly duo. The terrific twosome. The... perfect pair!'

'Yeah, that works actually. Race you home! I reckon I can beat your score on Alien Invasion 2, you know.'

'No chance!'

And off we ran, best friends, Big Mart and Charlie Custard, into the sunset. But it wasn't the end. It was just a new beginning.

Charlie Custard

Charlie Custard

Charlie Custard

Greg Dobbins has written several picture books and novels for children. If you've enjoyed this one, please do let him know!!

Twitter: @ThatGregDobbins

Facebook:
www.facebook.com/GregDobbinsWriter

It's the end. Put me down. Go and play outside. Ride your bike. Look at the clouds.

Maybe lend me to a friend!

Printed in Great Britain
by Amazon